CONTENTS

SOURCES

1 & 2. William Richardson, *The Pious Recreation: containing a New Sett of Psalm-Tunes, in Three Parts. With Six Hymns for the Use of Societies and Charity-children...* (London, 1729)

3. Martin Madan, *A Collection of Psalm and Hymn Tunes, never published before* [for the Lock Hospital] (London, 1769?)

4. *Psalms, Hymns & Anthems for the use of the children of the hospital for the maintenance and education of exposed and deserted young children* (London, 1774?)

5. *A Companion to the Magdalen-Chapel containing the Hymns, Psalms, Ode, and Anthems, used there, set for the Harpsichord, Voice, German-Flute or Guitar. The music composed by the most eminent masters* (London, 1780?)

6. ed. William Gawler, *The Hymns and Psalms used at the Asylum or House of Refuge for Female Orphans* (London, 1790?)

7. Maria Barthelemon, *Three Hymns, and Three Anthems composed for the Asylum, and Magdalen Chapels...* Op. 3 (London, [1795])

8. *Psalms, Hymns and Anthems for the Foundling Chapel* (London, 1796)

9 & 10. ed. John Page, *Collection of Hymns dedicated by permission to the Society of Patrons of the Anniversary of the Charity Schools in London and its environs* (London, 1804)

CHURCH MUSIC SOCIETY PUBLICATIONS RS149

General Editor: Geoffrey Webber

ASYLUM for female ORPHANS inftituted in the Year 1758.

JANE SAVAGE
(1752/3 – 1824)

Whilst shepherds watch'd their flocks by night

Hymn for Christmas Day
for Girls' Voices in unison and Organ

edited by
RACHEL WEBBER

CHURCH MUSIC SOCIETY

CHURCH MUSIC SOCIETY PUBLICATIONS RS154

General Editor: Geoffrey Webber

Solemn Notes of Sweetest Sound

Sacred music for upper voices & organ
from the Charity Institutions
for girls and boys in Georgian London

compiled and edited by
RACHEL WEBBER

CHURCH MUSIC SOCIETY

Amongst the many forgotten histories of music, the activities of the children who lived in the Charity Institutions of Georgian London are remarkable not only for the high level of musical accomplishment achieved but also for the equal involvement of girls as well as boys. Handel's generous support for the Foundling Hospital by allowing the profits from performances of Messiah to go to the Institution is well known, but the singing of the children themselves has largely been ignored. The nearest equivalent to have received attention is the singing of the girls at the Ospedali in Venice, thanks to the presence of Vivaldi as its Director of Music.

The children of the charity schools in London often sang at the local parish church, and came together for an annual massed-choir performance that was held from 1782 St Paul's Cathedral, an event famously praised by both Haydn and Berlioz on visits to London. The most ambitious regular singing of charity children was in the chapels of the charity institutions, which were often well attended by members of the public, including notable dignitaries such as Horace Walpole. Their music has largely been forgotten as it survives not in the manuscript and printed sources associated with the all-male choirs of the royal foundations and St Paul's Cathedral, but in publications issued by the charity institutions themselves, with contents ranging from simple hymns and psalms to extended anthems, occasionally by women composers.

The music in this collection comes from publications issued by the Asylum for Female Orphans (Lambeth), the Foundling Hospital (Bloomsbury), the Lock Hospital (Westminster), the Magdalen Hospital (Southwark), and two collections connected to the charity schools, one of which was prepared for the 1804 St Paul's festival. The hymns, psalms and anthems were mostly composed for one or two parts (often with various solo and tutti divisions) and organ, either just figured bass or fully written out, sometimes with solo introductions and interludes. The singing of the former prostitutes at the Magdalen chapel was famous for taking place in two separate galleries (where they sang from behind screens), and the charity school collections sometimes specified the singing of girls and boys both separately and together. The texts were often contemporary paraphrases of psalms of praise, seemingly chosen to inculcate a sense of gratitude in the children to their rescuers, giving thanks to God for the opportunity presented to them to improve their lives. Some specially written texts refer to the dire circumstances from which the children had been rescued, and are often concerned with praising the generosity of the charity's benefactors. These texts, such as the original text for the anthem by William Russell included in this collection, are not suitable for liturgical performance today, and so a completely different text (in the same metre) has been provided here for Russell's anthem.

This anthology, named after a phrase in Mr Green's anthem *Thou who art enthroned above*, includes some of the shorter pieces found in the publications, together with one extract from a longer anthem, for use as anthems or introits. It features music by several of the leading musicians of the period such as Thomas Arne and John Stanley, and reveals how it was evidently acceptable for women composers to find an outlet for their creativity in association with these institutions. Maria Barthelemon's collection of 1795 was composed for the Asylum and Magdalen chapels. Her husband, the Frenchman François-Hippolyte Barthélemon, made an edition and arrangement of a psalm by the fashionable Venetian composer Benedetto Marcello (previously published in an English version by John Garth in 1757) for the Asylum chapel. The pieces have also been selected to provide a variety of texts for use during the church's year. Jane Savage's setting of *Whilst shepherds watch'd their flocks by night* is available separately (see overleaf), and some of the more extended anthems from the repertoire are also being prepared for publication.

PERFORMANCE
Choir directors may wish to choose forces as appropriate for their circumstances rather than follow the particular indications shown here from the original sources. Decani and cantoris could be used, for example, instead of 'girls' and 'boys' in the opening piece of the collection. Flexibility can also be used in relation to the organ parts. It is not always clear, for example, whether continuo realisations should double or be independent from the vocal lines, or to what extent thinner or thicker textures or solo stops might be employed. Appoggiaturas should be played using the note value of the appoggiatura itself.

For a full critical commentary and editorial policy, see the Commentaries page of the CMS website (www.church-music.org.uk).

Rachel Webber
2022

Cover illustration: frontispiece in Jonas Hanway, *Reflections, essays and meditations on life and religion* (London, 1761), showing a Magdalen in her uniform outside the chapel entrance.

1. O God our Lord, how wonderful are thy works

Psalm 8, verses 1-2 (Thomas Sternhold)

William Richardson (dates unknown)
edited by Rachel Webber

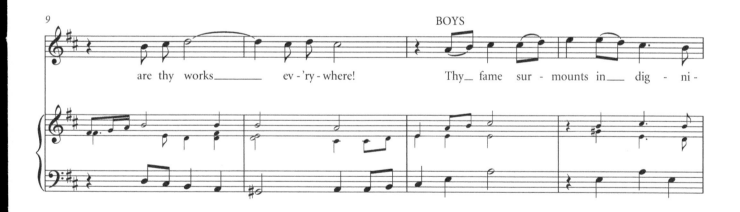

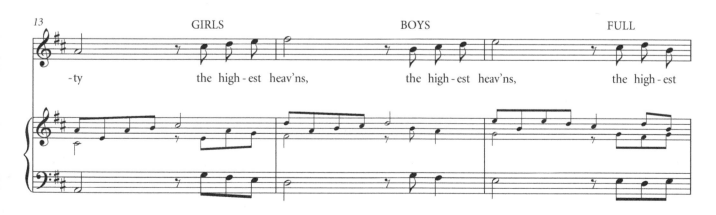

OXFORD UNIVERSITY PRESS, GREAT CLARENDON STREET, OXFORD OX2 6DP

2. How blest are they

Psalm 119, verses 1-4 (Tate and Brady)

William Richardson (dates unknown)
edited by Rachel Webber

Printed in Great Britain

OXFORD UNIVERSITY PRESS, GREAT CLARENDON STREET, OXFORD OX2 6DP

3. *Glory be to God on high*

Charles Wesley (1707-1788)

Jane Bromfeild (?) (dates unknown)
edited by Rachel Webber

4. Thou who art enthroned above

Psalm 92, verses 1-5 (George Sandys)

Mr Green (dates unknown)
edited by Rachel Webber

Printed in Great Britain

OXFORD UNIVERSITY PRESS, GREAT CLARENDON STREET, OXFORD OX2 6DP

CHORUS

5. *My God in whom are all the springs*

Isaac Watts (1674-1748)

Thomas Arne (1710-1778)
edited by Rachel Webber

Printed in Great Britain

OXFORD UNIVERSITY PRESS, GREAT CLARENDON STREET, OXFORD OX2 6DP

6. *O Lord our Governor*
(O di che lode)

Psalm 8, verse 1

Benedetto Giacomo Marcello (1686-1739)/
François-Hippolyte Barthélemon (1741-1808)
edited by Rachel Webber

Printed in Great Britain

OXFORD UNIVERSITY PRESS, GREAT CLARENDON STREET, OXFORD OX2 6DP

For the Anniversary at The Magdalen Hospital

7. Hide thy face from my sins

(first movement)

Psalm 51, verses 9-12

Maria Barthelemon (1749-1799)
edited by Rachel Webber

Printed in Great Britain

OXFORD UNIVERSITY PRESS, GREAT CLARENDON STREET, OXFORD OX2 6DP

blot out_ all mine i - ni - qui-ties,   mine i-

-ni - qui-ties.   Hide thy face__ from my sins,____ and

blot out all mine i - ni - qui-ties,   and blot out all mine i - ni - qui-ties.

(ad lib.)

8. Spirit of mercy, truth and love

Anonymous

John Stanley (1712–1786)
edited by Rachel Webber

CHORUS

And still from age to age___ con - vey, The won - ders of this sa - cred___ day.

SOLO

In ev - 'ry___ clime,___ in ev - 'ry___ tongue, Be God's e - ter - nal___ prais - es sung, Thro' all___ the___ list - 'ning___ earth___ be taught, The acts___ our great re -

9. *The Lord my pasture shall prepare*

Psalm 23 (Joseph Addison)

Charles Wesley (1757-1834)
edited by Rachel Webber

10. *How calm and beautiful the morn*

(Original text: To thee great God our thanks are due)

Thomas Hastings (1784-1872)

William Russell (1777-1813)
edited by Rachel Webber

OXFORD UNIVERSITY PRESS, GREAT CLARENDON STREET, OXFORD OX2 6DP

Now_ cheer - ful to_ the house_ of prayer_ Your ear - ly foot - steps, ear - ly foot - steps_ bend; The Sa - viour will_ him - self be there,_ Your ad - - vo - cate, and_ your friend:

Once by_ the_

law your hopes_____ were__ slain,__ But now in Christ ye____ live a -

- gain, once by the_____ law____ your____ hopes____ were____ slain,__ but

now_____ in____ Christ__ ye live_____ a - gain,__ but now in Christ__ ye

live__ a - gain.

a tempo giusto

CHORUS

How tran - quil now the ri - sing day! 'Tis

Je - sus still ap - pears, A - ri - sen

Lord to chase a - way Your

Church Music Society Publications
Music for Upper Voices issued on behalf of the Society by Oxford University Press
Sample pages of all titles are available on the Oxford University Press website

'Lamb of God'   CMS R99
Four motets for upper voices and organ by French and French-inspired composers of the late 19th and early 20th centuries: Léo Delibes (arr. Patrick), *Agnus Dei* (SA), Ernest Chausson, *Ave verum corpus* (S), Robert Meade, *Tantum ergo* (S), and Gabriel Fauré, *Salve Regina* (S).

Charles Gounod, *Noël*   CMS RS148a
For soprano and alto soloists, three-part upper voices and piano (with optional organ). The original scoring of Gounod's Christmas classic, with texts in French and English.

Jonathan Harvey, *The Tree*   CMS O8
A setting of verses from Job, mainly in unison but with some four-part writing, and organ, for general use.

Herbert Howells, *Magnificat and Nunc Dimittis in D* (1941)   CMS O21
Written for men's voices (mainly in unison, but with some divisi) and organ, but equally suitable for upper voices, this setting was composed for wartime use in Westminster Abbey.

Jane Savage, *Whilst shepherds watch'd their flocks by night* (ed. R. Webber)   CMS RS149
Anthem-style setting of the famous Christmas hymn for unison voices and organ, first published in 1785.

Peter Tranchell, *Bread of the world in mercy broken*   CMS O47
A setting of Bishop Heber's communion text for unison voices and organ (also with an arrangement for SATB).

Peter Tranchell, *Three Responsorial Psalms*   CMS O46
Settings of Psalms 15, 126 and 133 with refrains, for unison voices (upper or lower, or both) and organ. Also suitable as anthems for general use.

Paul Trepte & Patrick Russill (arr.) *Two Carols for Upper voices*   CMS O30
'Away in a manger' and 'Within the vale of Eden'. Arrangements of French traditional tunes for upper voices (dividing into three parts at times) and organ.

Stanley Vann, *Hail, true Body, born of Mary*   CMS O27
Short anthem for single voice or unison voices and keyboard, suitable for communion and Passiontide.

Samuel Wesley, *Two Sacred Songs* (ed. Langley/Webber)   CMS R90
'Gentle Jesus' and 'Might I in thy sight appear' for solo voice or unison voices and organ. Settings of texts by the composer's father, Rev. Charles Wesley, for general use.

Also available via the CMS website: www.church-music.org.uk
    Simon Lindley, *Courage,* for unison voices (with divisi) and organ
    Simon Lindley, *Salve Regina,* for unison voices (with divisi) and organ
    arr. Patrick Russill, *Infant holy,* for upper voices (two-part) and organ
    arr. Patrick Russill, *Rocking,* for upper voices (two-part) and organ

Origination by Jackie Leigh
Printed by Halstan & Co. Ltd, Amersham, Bucks.

ISBN 978-0-19-370794-8

Published on behalf of the Church Music Society by Oxford University Press,
Music Department, Great Clarendon Street, Oxford OX2 6DP

9 780193 707948